ENOUGH TO BE MORTAL NOW

poems

RIENZI CRUSZ

We acknowledge the support of the Canada Council for the Arts for our publishing program and the Government of Ontario through the Ontario Arts Council.

Canada Council for the Arts   Conseil des Arts du Canada

ONTARIO ARTS COUNCIL
CONSEIL DES ARTS DE L'ONTARIO

Cover design by Michael Crusz

Library and Archives Canada Cataloguing in Publication

Crusz, Rienzi, 1925-
Enough to be mortal now / Rienzi Crusz.

Poems.
ISBN 978-1-894770-60-6

I. Title.

PS8555.R87E56 2009 C811'.54 C2009-904814-0

Printed in Canada by Coach House Printing

TSAR Publications
P. O. Box 6996, Station A
Toronto, Ontario M5W 1X7
Canada

www.tsarbooks.com

CRITICAL PRAISE FOR RIENZI CRUSZ

If you want to share a sensibility which is at once primitive and sophisticated, both intense and subtle, a poetic craft which is taut and concentrated, then read *Flesh and Thorn.*

Quarry

Can Lit . . . has never articulated and transcended the experience of the incomer so wonderfully . . . the voice rings with a timbre known at once and altogether distinct; its range is abnormally large; its tone of infinite variety.

The New Quarterly

The cultural gift Crusz offers us, as a kind of magnificent verbal embroidery of plain cloth of Canadian speech, continually surprises, delights, mystifies, and liberates those of us raised on the sound of what Northrop Frye has called "the Canadian goose honk."

The Toronto South Asian Review

Arguably the best living Sri Lankan poet in English, though he has been in Canada since 1965, Crusz belongs to that older post-colonial generation, including such writers as Walcott and Soyinka, prepared to appropriate the colonial legacy of Shakespeare and English without anguished breast beating, "as a tongue to speak with."

World Literature Today

His "Immigrant's Song" is not only an attempt to come to terms with his own past, it is also a heroic statement of poetic independence.

Arun Mukherjee, *Currents*

Crusz, the most delicately nuanced (of such voices) uses his to balance a history, a role, and a difficult displacement . . . Like the West Indian poet, Derek Walcott [he] will not indulge in simplified opposition, whether of language, culture, or colour.

Ariel

Crusz's language is subtle and he makes his points obliquely. Moreover, his self-examination always includes the social context of an immigrant's struggle for a sense of identity.

Books in Canada

The Sun-Man poems are major artifacts of a new Canadian sensibility, important for the realities of our national selfhood.

Nancy Lou Patterson, University of Waterloo

Here was a true poetry of the displaced self, with sorrow beneath its bemused surface. Opposites—elephant and ice—are reconciled by a delightful wit, and ferocious though may be his interior heat, the light that the Sun-Man sheds upon the world lingers in the mind with a lovely after-glow.

Zulfikar Ghose, University of Texas

To call Crusz an immigrant poet is to summarize his intents too glibly. In both his books it is not the obvious contrast between elephant and rice, Sri Lanka and Canada, that is central but rather the manifold and specific ways in which a certain sensibility tries to cope honestly with perennial themes in both cultures.

Reshard Gool

A most articulate poetry, with a fascinating sense of where you come from and where to.

Robert Creely

His real genius lies not in the message contained in the poetry, but in the pursuit of perfection in poetic form. Very much a poet of sound and rhythm, Crusz writes with an awareness that poetry is about language, about the power of imagination. He is a very self-conscious poet, and that is precisely why his reputation will outlast that of his contemporaries.

Chelva Kanaganayakam, University of Toronto

For Anne
my beloved Muse,
and that lovable gang of four:
Daphne, John, Maria, and Michael

Enough to be mortal now . . .
—Tchicaya U Tam'si

There are no magics or elves
Or timely godmothers to guide us. We are lost, must,
Wizard a track through our own screaming weed.
—Gwendolyn Brooks

CONTENTS

The Edge of Silence

A Poetic Space

An Old Man's Scowl

In the Idiom of the Sun

These Other Configurations

The Edge of Silence

TIME/SNOWFALL

Time: soft as falling snow
Grows upon us, slowly,

seduces the landscape of eyes,
heart, bones' sleeping marrow;

and as we savour
this physics of whiteness falling,

this metaphor of innocence,
we also embrace the fireside warmth,

or ride the cold slopes
with limbs supple as bamboo,

forgetting the illusion,
until the rheumatism of bones,

congested lungs
hint at needles, scapel in gloved hands.

What's beneath time's
cruel fakery of snowfall

that eventually takes us by the hand
to our warm cradling couch,

TV's sunny metaphors
with *Roshan* our little *Coton-du-tulear*

sharing our happy death-watch.

BY THE EDGE OF THE MAHAVELI AT HIGH NOON

Why am I here   alone
by the edge of this great river?

The sun warm on my face,
hot air silent and pregnant;
the sun-fish sunning as usual,
a crow casting a long shadow on the waters
as if to spoil this promising day.

A lone heron casually alights
on the opposite bank   parades
her thin shapely legs, then bends
to seduce the minnows
as they surface like flotsam
under the noonday brilliance;

nothing breaks
the sentinel mood of the great river,
how sun-fish and minnow,
crow and heron,
high noon's lancing glare
the river's adamant quest
fashion this uncompromising story
with a happy ending:
the mighty river tumbling at last
into the ample arms of the Indian Sea.

So why and I here   alone
by the edge of this great river?

Searching for God
in this patch of green Eden?
answers in the baptism of waters,
silences to match
an empty cathedral?
Realities of life and death

in the heron's beak,
faith, like the river,
at journey's end?

My dark moments   dissolving
by the edge of the Mahaveli
at high noon.

THE FIREFLIES ARE WINKING TONIGHT

Never mind the fireflies
failing yesterday's August night,
the trembling fawn
frozen
before the truck's lightning eyes;
never mind the forsythia
discovering death
in its moments of yellow glory,
the summer catalpa
its winter nakedness.

I still rise
with morning on my face
take in the good earth
even though its bloodied bones
show through the morning snow;
I loaf through this mall's urgent crowd,
breathe in the promise
of its food-court air,
love as yesterday
with gentle words, limbs
that still keep their Lambada rhythms.

A falling grey hair
suggests time's cruel harvest,
a trim plot of graveyard,
but like the river that zings its way
to the waiting sea,
I keep singing, and singing
and singing

and the fireflies are winking tonight.

IN PRAISE OF SILENCE

Talk of silence
  and thunder and zigzag lightning
hits the mind first—
  then you, you with the mouth
that does not speak,
  but gently nudged,
and I hear your whispering to the roses
  on the mantel vase.

Left alone, untouched,
  there's thunder lurking in your bones,
the oyster of heaven waiting to be shucked;
  embrace you
and the spirit hovers
  as over the stillness of the cloister.

Silence,
  you are the belladonna
in all its exotic majesty,
  as deadly, as the soundless poison
that races through its veins,
  and another desperate man
stains his lonely room
  with blood and gun smoke.

Oracle
  in a capuchin cowl of silence
with wisdom hard as stone,
  answers for our dark foibles,
new epiphanies
  to change the scowl on our faces.

Silence, you are the Christ
  on the waters
that calms
  our frightened minds,

convulsive limbs, idiot laughter;
 who makes sense
of the chaos, the flotsam
 of all our pain.

The stillness of patience,
 waiting, waiting
for the God who looks
 on the noise of the world
as its death rattle,
 who'll only come
when the doors are closed for silence, ready
 for the Pentecostal light
of His divine candles.

ELEGY #2

Morning. Black hammering of crow
trying to tell me something?

Sudden magpie   alone
promising sorrow to wear on my face.

That same night, I heard the jak-tree owl hoot
from its darkened throat.

Cats took the parapet wall and caterwauled
their psalms for the dying.

Father, you died with morning on your face,
fulfilling the prophecies of birds.

I, rocked in the hammock of the sun,
your gentle ways,

refused the dark harbingers,
saw nothing

in the sliced face of the moon,
the broken reservoirs of your heart,

only believed   the God
on your wizened face,

your love   now silent
and hard as wood.

ANATOMY OF FEAR

Like cowled winter men
in cotton underwear, we move warm
in our own skins;
against the hunting world outside
we have mantras
that name, mark boundaries.

Like animals,
we pee on markers,
call the spaces within
our own civilized cells
with pink sunken baths,
pulsating shower heads,
brats, cars like sensuous women,
our own swath of green grass.

Beyond the tree line,
some other animal scent intrudes;
peripheries tremble with provocation,
suggest blood.
We thrive best
in the cage of our own smell.

Why minutiae grow like fungi,
the leaf buds   the tree dies;
we trade the living peacock
for one exotic feather,
slow twilight under stars
for the havocking moment,
sun
for lightning's crooked filament,

All mankind
for me   alone and afraid.

A PRAYER

Lord,

before I am born,
flood the waters of the womb with the colours of Your world:

the purulent wound, splattered blood,
giggling children on their hopscotch bases;

those with canticles in their mouths,
cathedrals in their hearts,

those that host the screaming demons
in their hollow heads;

before I learn to laugh
let me learn how to cry,

that next to the sweet mango tree
grows the dark babul.

Before I exult, utter the hooray word,
let me in on failure's hanging rope,

the stabbing moment, the sepulchered meditation
on life and death.

Before I can dig into this curried feast,
let me hold out the tin cup on some busy street,

learn hunger's embracing grip,
the utter coldness in the extremities.

Before I reach home
detour me on the refugee's mapless journey,

his lost children,
the charred home;

before you show me death's harvest of white bones,
show me life in the joyous flight of the goshawk.

SERMON IN THE FOREST

Weary,
the Buddha laid himself down
under the shade of a huge bo tree
and closed his eyes to the flame of sun
still spearing through
the lattice of leaves.

Now only the sounds
of the great forest
would sing through his ears,
and he must listen,
for he was still
on his long journey to Nibbhana.

So the Buddha listened:
to the dance of the bo leaves   rustling,
pivoting on their thin green stems, beating
their metallic song
on a guitar of wind;

to the rust-winged woodpecker   tattooing
its heartbeat on the gnarled ribs
of a jak tree, hammering
gathering the breath of life
with each beakfull of insect bones;

to a rock squirrel   belching,
stripping the mango flesh to the bone, dripping
the yellow juice on its tiny feet;
to the cawing, cawing
of a raven   relaying
the muffled cries of a fawn   trashing
in a hunting panther's throat.

And in the distance,
the rumble of elephant feet,

shiver and shake of jungle   parting
to the curling trunks   trumpeting,
bending and breaking the bones
of leaf and twig, cracking
the round skulls of woodapple,
and sucking their sweet marrow dry.

Then the Buddha
said to his disciple:
Listen to the sounds of the great forest,
how they rise and fall, the charades
of life and death;
but none of these living things
can climb out of their skulls,
or silence their cries of joy or pain,

only you, my son, can turn your red tongue to stone,
seek the silences   beyond
the laughter and tears in your bone,
and like
            the silent grass
            the silent fruit
            the silent sap
            of each living tree
find life in the silence of Nibbhana.

ROOTS

for Cleta Nora Marcellina Serpanchy

What the end usually demands
is something of the beginning,
and so
I conjure history from a cup
of warm Portuguese blood
from my forefathers
black diamond eyes, charcoal hair
from my Sinhalese mothers;
the beached catamaran,
gravel voices of the fishermen,
the catch still beating like a heart
under the pelting sun;
how the pariah dogs looked urgent
with fish-meal in their brains,
the children romped, sagged,
then melted into the sand.

A Portuguese captain holds
the soft brown hand of my Sinhala mother.
It's 1515 AD,
when two civilizations kissed and merged,
and I, burgher of that hot embrace,
write a poem of history
as if it were only the romance
of a lonely soldier on a crowed beach
in Southern Ceylon.

HOMECOMINGS

Tell me
  of that river
that hugs the monsoon rain
  takes in the fleeing flood
like a prodigal child,
  smoothes the boulder's jagged face
that juts along its way;

kisses each piece
  of passing driftwood like a blessing;
home to the crocodile's cruising snout,
  primordial jaws, the minnows
that seek the morning sun like a prayer,
  and I'll tell you why
there's no frown, no fog
  that ever stays over the river's laughing face▯
it knows of home, the journey's end,
  where from and where to,
that the mothering sea   awaits
  with pounding heart
for its prodigal return.

I've meandered
  this way and that,
from shore to shore, one love
  to another, blue skies to cumulus cloud▯
under an umbrella of doting children,
  still going   unafraid   laughing,
the blood fevering like some mischievous child▯
  always knowing the beginning,
the journey's throbbing walk
  to this igloo of heaven
or that sun-faced island of the elephant
  where I'm always at home,
if not home.

A Poetic Space

I AM NOW BALANCING ON ICE WITH A POEM IN MY HAND

for Dad

All agreed
that the omens at my birth were good:
the cow calved within minutes
of my arrival, the caretaker
spoke of udders
hanging from a full moon;

the old gardener cried *saddhu* to the sun
for turning his roses redder than blood,
though he couldn't understand
why their thorns were longer
and sharper this year;

the maid giggled into the veranda
with six warm eggs cupped in her hands,
first offerings
of the black leghorn pullets;
the family astrologer scaled me in Libra,
promising creative juices
strong as the currents of the Mahaveli;

my mother remarked
that I seemed to have danced in her womb,
and the fat midwife froze
when she slapped my buttocks
and heard my furious cheering.

Only my father was silent,
holding the joy and the torment of the omens
in his eyes,
and, having witnessed the first poem,
silently wondered
when and where, if ever,
I would fashion my others.

CONVERSATIONS WITH GOD ABOUT MY PRESENT WHEREABOUTS #2

for Chelva

In the end
it's a matter of canon—
their Holy of Holies,
a poetic held tight
in their big fists.

What flag did they see me wave
on my masthead,
Elephant or Ice?

Neither, they argued,
suggesting instead
runaway metaphors
for my vagrant immigrant feet.

OK. So I'm the separate one,
dancing on the cusp
of two worlds,
sitting on my haunches in no man's land
fashioning my exotic mythologies.

What to do
with this genie let out of his bottle?
Deconstruct him, they cried. Classify,
let him bear the vivisectionist's knife—
the Temple's veil must not be sundered.

But what about the "madness of art,"
mythologies without frontiers,
my hybridity's chameleon eyes,
the cross-bred rose
stewing in it fiesta colour?

And my Canadian effusions?

"I'm now snow-bank child, bundled,
with snot under my nose,"
my prayer "for the white slopes,
skimming, skidding skis,
torches, stars, brandy in the hot chocolate,"
my thoughts on "this igloo of heaven,"
"my brown laughing face in the snow"?

True. Like an acrobat on the high wire
who needs to flaunt his skill
and also stay alive,
I also sought "the sun-faced land of the elephant,"
where I could laze under a na tree,
suck the sweet rambuttan dry
or hear the raven caw, caw, caw
its daily prophecies.

Consider journeys,
ignore time's cruel markers,
beginnings, ends;
I tried speaking to them
of comings without goings
the immigrant's searching heart,

how the landscape changes,
the heartbeat alters its rhythms,
the stark beauty of a life
that like the sand dunes at dawn
offer only changing horizons,
chameleon shades.

They want closure,
clues to where the bodies can be found—
I offer my walking nowhere feet,
a pair of syncretic eyes.
For neat taxonomies,
I have contraries,
subversions, the paddy bird

in cardinal's feathers,
a returning for a going,
a going for a returning.

If I speak of elephant as poet,
I also draw his massive legs,
the snorting and breathing,
the thick froth in his mouth
as he hauls the huge logs
through jungle paths.

If I promised "the elephant and the raven
to sing their metaphors without compromise,"
I haven't forgotten "Colombo's walking dead,"
or "Pettah's shacks crumbling in the rain."

Lord, the journey's still on:
I'm still going, still "becoming"
always going, never arriving—
born of the "Burgher embrace
of a lonely soldier on a southern beach in Ceylon,
when two civilizations kissed and merged,"

how can I do the "dangerous thing"
and still live?
How do I "dance in this rarefied air"?

THE *KOHA* SINGS ONLY IN SEASON

for Abdul Lodhi

Those long silences—
time when darkness closed
the windows of earth,
the nightly spangle of stars
and the mind stopped wondering, searching
for the truth behind
our cobwebbed lives, the joys
of our sunlight days;

when night's dark distemper
shadowed the jambu tree in the backyard
and turned its vermilion fruit
to nothing but a spray of obsidian eyes;
how the paddies once golden in the sun
now swayed in their thin charcoal bones;

when the river that laughed
and chased after with lusty arms
the open sea
could no longer hide
its now wrinkled face from the raven
and shared its karma with a lone elephant dead
by the waterless edge;

when the words would not come,
my metaphors flounder
and my thoughts look like naked manikins;
when the poem would not write, the song
would not sing,
when my friend Abdul Lodhi
lost his life too soon, too soon
and I wasn't ready to write his elegy.

The *koha* sings only in season.

Cuckoo bird of morning song,
trumpeter
to the Sinhala new year
you leave the night
to the guttural throat of the *bukamoona*;

gone the memories
of the surgeon's knife,
morphine's dull bandage of pain
it's the morning of a new day,
and I'll light the candles again, one by one,
pitch my canticles to high heaven,
and hitch my new words
to the rhythms of the Kandyan drums, the *baila* song.

Abdul Lodhi, I am writing your elegy at last.

bukamoona: Sri Lankan fish owl
baila: type of music and dance first introduced by the Portugese to Sri Lanka

POETRY BEHIND BARS

The big cats behind bars.

Stand back,
watch the kingdoms in their smoking eyes,
limbs, how they move liquid
against the cage's cold ribs,
the dream
still hot in their chained muscles.

How Gemunu, the Bengal tiger,
crouches (as before the final leap)
and even now in sleep
turns these grey bars
to tall blonde grass;

Kutti, the black panther,
shuts out the white moon
with his charcoal skin
as he sets fire to a wild pig
with diamond-torch eyes;

and Sheba, the old lioness,
takes back the Serengetti plains
from limb to zebra limb
with a single bellowing roar.

These are all ghosts, ghosts
of poems, imperial, revisited.
If you want the substantive thing,
the primeval dance of fire
let the animals out
one by one.

Then will you gather
no blur of words, pablum,
deconstruction's frail white bones,

only raw feelings   meanings
leaping with life and death,

art
which is "to do the dangerous thing".

POEM FOR THE FALTERING MAN

I'm balancing
on the brink

death and panorama
around and below.

But faltering legs
dangerous landscape

or final decisions
will not make the poem.

Only the supreme electricity
of doubt,

those screaming moments
when wind, muscle, and mind

argue
whether to keep me up here

alive.

RIENZI . . .

for Michael Estok

"Rienzi,
sometimes the master
learns from the pupil"
—Love, Mike

What have you learnt from me,
professor, mon ami?
The poet on the cover of your book
poses with the abandon
of a banion,
you looking like a young Keats
drinking up the sun.

I read your poems:
"Chansons Acadiennes",
"Spells and Curses",
"the desperate solidarities"—
all lean and muscled like stallions, nowhere
near my fat sun, my hefty words,
my wounds red as immortelle.

So what have you learnt, Sir?
You who sing nothing but the polished stone,
the exact chirrup of a dying cricket,
the subtle magic in the prairie's face
and always the kernel, the kernel,
husk and shell out on the rubbish heap.
All this genius, yours not mine.

I broke all the rules—
the sun chattering in my teeth,
my hair on fire,
the smell of elephant,
body and brain listening all the while
to the mad and seering order of words.

When I coloured, I coloured wildly,
feather of Ibis, the sun

with blood on its face.
When I killed, I mauled them to sleep,
could never shoot clean between the eyes.
The extravagant metaphor always mine,
mine like honey in the mouth.

POETICS FOR THE DOUBTING ONE

Yes—mine are stories
to storm your walnut eyes,
make light your serious head.

How away from the mauling sun
I squat under a *murunga* tree
and wait—for Puspa, my favourite mother elephant,
to come along and discuss family affairs,
hers and mine;

wait for Shakunta, the mammoth tusker
to lay me down gently
and extract my painful wisdom tooth.
Refuse your invading thoughts:
my mental gibberish, the sun's suffusing madness?

OK, so I also dismiss prophecies:
your two magpies suddenly darting from nowhere
and alighting on my left shoulder;
no ears either
to your cats wailing on the parapet wall,
or the raven's raucous cry from the jambu tree.
Granted,
my beloved father died under similar omens.

Why do I laugh
seeing you walk barefooted
in a white sari to the temple
to listen to the old monk
recite his *seth kavi*
for your father's return to his family?

Why refuse the magic
of your house-warming rituals,
the pot of milk boiling over
to sign the kitchen floor?

Woman, if you can walk with the superstitious stars
bound to your shapely ankles,
let the intransigent moon
havoc in your storm of curls
birds speak in tongues
of hollow oracles,

why can't you for once say yes
to the god of imagination,
madness that can pirouette on a pinhead
and believe:
an elephant that's a superb psychiatrist,
another that thinks
he's a professional dentist?

Listen. At the margins of poetry
are lies, modes of ridicule,
foul words, sweet nothings;
but savour the mad beautiful dance of metaphor,
imaginative leaps, primeval chaos—
for at the centre
lies truth
still and uncompromising as desert stone.

•

THE CHILD WHO WOULD BE A POET

for Michael

High expectation—
  his mother praying
that at last her son would cross
  that first threshold of civilization,
sit on his brand now potty
  and quietly shit away his pablum.

High expectation—
  his father's fervent hope
that his son would gently go
  with his mother's exhortations,
discipline his bowel movements
  and reduce the pamper bill
to zero.

Secretly
  (without a twitch of muscle)
the old poet exults
  as his son quickly arranges
the shining white bowl on his head
  and parades the room duly hatted.

Both father and mother
  now seemed to understand
the true nature
  of art, childhood, and violence,
as a new and disturbing poem
  havocs in mother's incredulous eyes.

THERE'S ALWAYS A WATER BEAD IN THE CACTUS

for my favourite students at SSAS

Daily,
come sun or rain,
snow or sleet,
Muse under your legs or nowhere,
you write, write for two hours.
So instructed the old poet.

Keep squeezing   squeezing
till something spills—
The stone will eventually give, perspire,
there's always a water bead
in the cactus.

Relax. Let your muscles,
your mind
take off like a butterfly.
Patience, even if
you must pick your nose,
there's always a nugget
in the gumbo of words.

If the poem is shaping
to zero,
if the doodles, lines
are without geometry,
words without arms, legs or eyes,
if you cannot find
the heart of the poem

and everything looks
like the weather report: heavy cloud,
cold, windy,
precipitation 85%,

then tomorrow

tomorrow   the poem
tomorrow   the truth.

LIKE A HOUND DOG

The word
hunts the poet—
dark alleys
smoky pubs
blonde corn fields
rice paddies sizzling in the sun,
wherever;

conjures
a cemetery
of dead autumn leaves
of his front-yard catalpa undressing
to winter's fierce gaze
or his pet dog, Sparky, leaping
from its ashes
on the fireplace mantel,
whatever;

or the poet, the word?

In either case
there is a killing
and a resurrection
like the Digger wasp
that paralyzes the spider
lays a single egg
in its belly
and waits patiently
for its waspy poem

THE ELEPHANT WHO WOULD BE A POET

High noon. The piranha sun
cuts to the bone.
Anula, the heaving elephant
froths from the mouth.
The logging ends.

Without a command
he eases his huge body to the ground,
rolls over,
and makes new architecture
with his thick legs,
four columns vertical
to the sun.

The confused mahout
refuses the poem in this new equilibrium
this crazy theatre of the mind,

this new way
of looking at the world,
upside down.

7 WAYS OF LOOKING AT A POET

1.
Yes. He is the same man
  you saw last morning at the Coffee Shoppe
in the company of a doughnut, hot coffee, and a cigarette,
  but one you do not see at night
sipping cold coffee and hunting for words
  to sing of the cobwebbed symmetry of stars,
loafing fireflies, babies
  bawling in their mothers' arms,
of gun smoke, raven, and elephant,
  curve of buttock, lovers
under a blue moon, refugees
  dying in the Darfur sun.

2.
Demosthenes
  with stones in his mouth
who turns his stammering beginnings—
  his boisterous duel with bugger words,
intrusive images,   those
  with bare-faced lies in their bones,

to the eventual magic
  of profound words, resounding rhetoric.

3.
Who first sees the world,
  a blob, a blur,
then clearly as daylight
  as he discovers its heartbeat
on the kitchen table—
  the upside-down bottle of ketchup,
water glass, pepper, and salt,
  the fruit bowl of apples
waiting patiently for their juicy deaths.

4.
How he crosses a frontier
  in search of a new Jerusalem,
matches his tumultuous soul
  against howling winds, ravaging cold,
a thick shroud of snow,
  to grasp his immigrant dream
without ever forgetting
  the small cabook house
where he was born—
  the flame of bougainvillea
on this back yard fence,
  his kingdom of raven and elephant.

5.
He's the one
  who first imagines God
as only in the solitude of the cloister,
  under the Capuchin's soutane,
somewhere in the swirling incense
  of the cathedral's high altar,
then finds Him
  amidst a rollicking crowd
in the Village Fair,
  in the face of a grandpa standing by
a Ferris wheel of laughing children.

6.
Who discovers
  the emptiness of words,
the ugly face of fakery,
  in his narrative of the fishermen of Sri Lanka
shaped from photographs,
  his dictionary of words, jaded facts
from the computer's cold mouth,
  after he meets an old man
sitting on a boulder in Mt Lavinia's beach,
  with salt in his fisherman's veins,

and a true mouthful of fables
  about the catamaran men of the Indian sea.

7.
Yes, he's the one born screaming
  with a poem in his throat,
who learns the rhythms of words
  from Mother Goose fables
on his mother's knee,
  keeps faith in the dance of words
through his stallion, summer years,
  and when life's autumn comes,
and winter blows

writes the poem
  he has become.

HOW TO DANCE IN THIS RAREFIED AIR

How he jabs his thick forefinger
  into my poetic
as if it were a breastbone.
  O God, how it hurts:

cups his eyes
  against my passionate burning,
the bougainvillea's profusion,
  elephant
as rogue in heat.

My words, it would seem,
  elude him by a generation;
I would walk only
  in shaded byways or exotic arbours,
the poem jaundiced
  without the blood of a new idiom.

What he wants
  is wasteland:
white, scrubbed, frontier;
whose poems
  must deconstruct to bare bone,
the flesh and blood laid out separate
  to dry like fish
in the noonday sun.

No. I will not desert
  those wintered killing fields,
the spilled blood sweeter
  among the paddies, the frangipani,
upside-down elephant
  squinting at the sun.
Noble Eliot, you might as well
  rest in peace,
your ransom will not be paid.

My ear to the ground
  and I hear the drumbeat of Avon,
mad Hamlet strut and nurse
  his eloquent pain;
Milton, hammering Lucifer
  to a perfect poetic, a perfect Hell.

Wounded,
  give me the psalms of David,
words to learn by rote,
  comfort the dark sargassum
of my days,
  how the Valley of Death
passes like a bad dream.

I am still here, Montes de Oca,
  my beautiful wild Mexican bard,
belting my boisterous song;
  and Pablo, hug me again,
show me the true metaphors
  of sun and rain,
how to throw my bread on the waters,
  circle the world with a poem.

Speak to me, Rabindranath,
  I need to hear your distant voice,
bask under your stunning skies;
  and Kahlil, I haven't forgotten
your wisdom that must laugh
  and weep, bow one's head to a child.

And Dylan, do I ever love the melody
  of your song, your riotous book of words;
good Manley, sing, sing, sing,
  I'm all ears and silent;
Lorca, my friend,
  tell me the secrets of "Duende,"
ask the spirit to stab my words again.

Rilke, take me gently
  into the depths of myself,
the soundless paths,
  how to listen, listen, listen;
as for you, Vallejo,
  teach me the thunder of silence,
the value of the spilled blood,

how to dance in this rarefied air.

An Old Man's Scowl

ONLY THE GESTURE, MY LOVE

for Anne

Love, if you wish to say to me:
"I love you darling"
don't!
Just hug me
and let our bodies
explode your words
in utter silence.

What would you rather have?

Words
with the heart of the chameleon,
parables with no clear answers,
narratives that often dance
on the cusp of truth and falsehood,
the sometimes guttural noise of their stories

or

truth
in the uncompromising gesture:
a dimpled smile,
an old man's scowl,
a clenched fist,
a grandma with open arms,
a child's sneaky hands in the cookie jar,
a hug
that trumps the fire of words?

BANQUET FOR MY COLONIAL MASTERS

Gauguin's woman under another sun
raped. How silence spilled
from an abattoir of tongues.

How your freighters cough black,
then guffawed and left heavy
with coconut and tea,
cardamom, cinnamon, and ivory,
the sandalwood artifacts
still leaking their exotic perfume
from their dark holds.

And through it all
I heard the Englishman's siesta snore,
the civilized cooing
of civilized men
gulping their velvet whiskies,
as brown waiters bent and bowed
to the evening noise of their masters.

And you still show me
your polished banisters,
your country estates,
green, columned, and groomed.

So what was left to keep?
Shakespeare!
a tongue to speak with,
some words to remember.
Today,
we are all poets
for having suffered the chains,
for having learnt the language.

IF YOU MUST KEEP YOUR PARADISE

for John

Go, my son, go
as a gentle summer breeze, or
if you must, an autumn gust,
and in time, the world will go along with you

as your walking shoes
take on the certain rhythm of the stars.

Live your life, my son,
without those dark moments
trying   to understand;

walk by the roses
exploding in your yard, saffron of forsythia,
or stand beneath the catalpa's perfect umbrella;
then step out of your gazebo eyes
into the frail nakedness
of your favourite Rose of Sharon
the exotic peonies' crumpled remains,
your white ghost of lawn

and ask not
of how or why, about
their seasons of life and death,
the metronome beat of their living;
and if you wear your elephant ears
you'll hear the king maple whispering
its eternal song: I grow in innocence
of my growing. I have no questions or answers.

If you walk down the street
you'll often meet
those other faces, mouths,
sunburnt hands   fevering
to the bedlam music

of their gestures, words, but
listen carefully and you'll hear
your precious blood thundering red through their veins;

embrace the darkness
as you would the comforting sun;
laugh from the belly, or cry
as the raven over its fallen kind
but don't ever be another Adam
and lose your paradise, your mortal angels,
by hanging your head
and trying to understand it all.

PRAYER #2

Save me, Lord,

from the land that lost
its pot of milk and honey,

that now only sighs
through dry cracked ribs,

whose mighty river
sings and suns no more;

save me

from the smile
that asks for something I cannot give,

from the man
who thinks he's treading water

as he sways from side to side
on bamboo stilts;

save me

from those critics
who suck the pablum of understatement,

cringe at the poem
of dripping blood and raw meat;

save me

from the crooked shadows
of myself,

those moments

when even the gargoyles begin to weep,

as I wrestle the demon of words and wait
for the end of my cruel banishment,

that stifling darkness,
that thundering and rolling

just before my spring awakening.

GOD AMONG THE MALL WALKERS

Slow   in my own arthritic style,
I've just managed to cover two rounds of the course—
five is the accepted distance
for oiling the ageing joints, raising the heart rate,
and faking a smile at the roadrunners
who burn up the miles like a rich boy's Miata.

Forget the six and seven rounders,
I can only manage four.
Ankles now heavy as lead,
walking has turned to hobbling,
as the leg muscles tighten and cry for help.
Forget about faking a smile
at the roadrunner showoffs,
in another life
I would have opted for a quick killing.

Lord, when did you come up with this idea
of a walking geriatric hospital?
Look at them: Mr McIver desperately trying
to pump up his heart
with rounds of slow motion;
Maria Dupont seems to stumble every few feet,
the rumour being that her inner ear
is painfully unhappy.

Dennis Mumford of 76+
and enlarged prostrate
attemps to strut like a teenager.
And what of Sparky Cosmo?
The roadrunner with a crooked smile
and severe arthritis in both knees?

But, as if to fashion a fine balance, contradict
this parade of twilight men,
lovely young Maria Ponzanelli flashes by,

the Lord's happy therapy
of flopping blond hair, firm breasts and swaggering buttocks,
to stir the blood-beat.

And Lord, how you cleverly shift the scene
from slow-moving bodies on corridors
to the Food Court turned Tim Horton's;
gossip and laughter, the stock market blues,
terrorism, coffee and doughnuts, old men retired happy
with money bags bulging in their vaults;
the wives happily bunched together,
as if time and coffee break
has no end.

SOLITUDE #2

I thought
you were the god of loneliness

halo without light
cold temple with no oil lamps

craggy geography
where footsteps rarely sing

only searching men
who seek the Divine.

I thought
you were a den of fallen leaves

closed, secret
as the graveyard of the elephant

a stage for mourning
a silence before sorrow

a silence after sorrow
a metaphor of bones.

And you said: come naked
bring no burden or baggage

only thoughts   empty
as a sun-ravaged waterhole

eyes in black blindfold
ears lingering in the prison

of the deaf
the music unheard unsung.

Only then solitude's gypsy tambourines
fireside carnival

stupas (once dead under jungle vine)
shimmering like Christmas trees

the land   flat and open
as the prairies

blonde cornfields diamond sun
scythe music on the reaping shore

poetry shivering through
solitude's thunder and lightning.

THE MAN WITH TWO FACES

You like thin
  catwalk parade
  of lean muscle, buttock, and long legs
  answering your scrounging eyes;
  I like fat
  the slow body in slow motion
  elephant amble   coconut breast   an arm that rises slowly
  like a shy moon
  a poetry of body in excess:

You like hair,
  a blondness shaking over slim neck
  or charcoal head to match the raven;
  I like bald, the new-born mode,
  clean pate, uninterrupted space
  ready for the sun, her soft fingers;

You like the eagle
  its giant wing span, x-ray eyes
  a kingdom without argument;
  I like the raven, its mathematical head,
  the cawing harbinger of the dying, the birthing, the feasting,
  the world's other newspaper;

You like snow
  its signature of innocence, arctic skin,
  the thrill in your skis, promise
  of hot chocolate, the sand-box child's snowman;
  I like the sun, bronze face
  that's like my own, the mango ripening
  in its womb, the ultimate light driving out
  the tormentors of night   a warmth
  sweetheart to arthritic bone;

You like things   gadgets
  fridge with it cool steel face

singing kettle, TV's plasma face;
I like what's behind—
the searching mind   crouched over drawing board
formulas crawling in his notebooks
the noise of his eureka screams;

You like the throbbing Mall
with discounts in your face
sound of the salesgirl's urgent pitch
the Food Court's chatter
its happy throng taking in the smell of New York Fries
like incense at Sunday Vespers;

I like solitude
those ample spaces of loneliness
the thunder of silence
or if it be sound
let it be the sound of poetry
Dylan Thomas after his barrel of beer
leaning over his lectern
and caressing my ears with his symphony of words.

But listen
you are no different from me
I am you
in different season, in another mood,
that other side of you is me,
that other side of me is you—

So, let's hold hands and dance
the snow is falling, the sun is up,
the eagle has spread its wings
the raven's hosting a party for his tribe
at the city dump,
and by nightfall the stars will move again
in their perfect geometries.

HOMESCAPES

1.
She used to spend hours in the kitchen:
my wife spreading the menu on Sunday afternoon
from pappadams to salmon patties;
add *temperado* rice, beef curry
hot as chillies,
and you have bonanza,
a stomach perfect
for the Sunday afternoon snooze.

Come Christmas,
and I play Santa Claus
with a microwave oven, a cookbook to match.
She quickly converts to the lean cuisine,
throws in the chicken-legs dinner,
and smiles feeling
leaner and leaner.

2.
As a child,
I frolicked about the Wellawatte beach,
washed my morning face in the Indian Sea;
talked to the crabs, then stampeded them
to their graves in the golden sand;
rubbed my legs with seaweed,
hugged the warming sun
as sea water caressed my twiddling toes.

Early dawn,
and I've combed the woods behind our *cabook* house,
picked up after the fruit bats:
sweet mango, olive, the juicy *cadju-pulang*:
then off to the loft in the barn
to suck the honey fruits.
Under his mouth
a bowl of cereal,

his teaspoon playing the loops of corn;
close to hand his instruments of distraction,
three shining "gobots" ready
for their sweet unravelling;
above his curly head, the presence:
his mother, now visibly shaken by the slipping day,
this untidy feat
of childhood stalling.

FOR A POET FRIEND TRASHED BY A "HUMBLING WIND"

After reading your poem enclosed
in your letter of September 4, 2006,
I sketched Golgotha
on its white margins—
and the "humbling wind" came again,
but the hanging tree refused
to give up its hero.

Once again,
lightning knifed the earth,
made fire in the chalice of the lily,
scythed Roman knees in shame,
but the naked man hung still,
the triumph of nailed body to wood.

My friend, listen
to the hard poem in pain:
the stone sings in its solid prison,
the bog, shifting sands,
carry their deaths
in small murmurs of song.

If you have no altar,
make one, the harder the better.
Pain is like the hanging tree,
a vantage point that looks at darkness,
conjures the Golgotha Man
trembling in his triumph,
bruised hardness
who is first to know, feel,
see the resurrection.

APARTMENT #13

As if to parade
  gestures
of a summer without end,
  this butterfly pirouettes
on the couch, kisses
  the hanging Boston fern,
flirts wildly with the window sheers,
  and takes off
into the framed blue sky.

No hint of death
  primed in her pin bones,
the sumac, it seems,
  will flame for ever
and summer's lusty dance
  has no thought
of Fall's coming doom.

So I,
  once slave to signs and metaphors,
interpreter of dreams
  who trembled each time the cats wailed
on the parapet wall,
  deny this numerology of doom:
I rent apartment # 13
  and thrive: my children,
  profession, poetry,
all taking giant leaps.

But #13 spun their minds:
  the Super now treats me
as if I was born under a mongoloid moon:
  the Avon Lady shudders
each time she passes my #13 way,
  and the Electrolux salesman walks quickly by,
convinced there's a jinx, no money

behind the sigil door.

Never mind the rumours
of possible ghosts—
the school teacher
who took the barbiturate way;
how an 80-year-old man
angered by the meter reader
for breaking his siesta,
burst out of his #13 door,
and reshaped the man's face
with his gnarled cane.

I'm going along
with the gypsy butterfly,
the adamant sumac,
summer's carnival face,
and refusing
the dark superstitions on my front door,
will laugh and dance, dance and laugh
to Heaven's brief music
behind my #13 door.

SLOW DANCING

for Kingsley

When I stagger each morning into the promise of the day,
sit patiently till the going of the sun;

when I see no stories, revelations, fireflies
in the night's hard shadows;

when the city's noonday glare
gives up nothing but hobo clothes, a teen's unloved eyes;

when I pump my heart every fourth hour
with Maxwell House coffee,

and swear by God
on vitamin E, and B-Complex;

when the headlines in my newspaper
seem like old hat,

and I keep to the ads for topsoil,
handymen, tree cutters, and window washers;

when my once dancing feet no longer hear
the tango's gypsy rhythms, the kaffrinja beat,

and I take to the shuffle's slow exertions,
a music plucked from Welk's cotton candy bag;

when like a prayer the menu
comes up with fish and veggies and no dead meat,

and the fridge holds Heavenly Hash
like a forbidden fruit;

when the kneecaps are worn,
and cataracts have smoked the eyes,

and the kingdom of God is at hand,

then know this, my friend,
I'm in the twilight of my bones,

slow dancing.

NOTES OF A SAINT SUFFERING FOR A SINNER

After the surgeon's knife,
four and a half hour's anaesthetic sleep,
morphine nights of wild dreams,
where pain is the prow of your face,
and your 4 hospital brothers
parade their decaying veins of death,
a sinner takes unearned warmth,
a sliver of hope
from a saint:

> *All the works of God proceed slowly and in pain,*
> *therefore their roots are sturdier*
> *and their flowering lovelier*
> —Mother Theresa

THE TROUBLE WITH GROWING OLD

is not living (slowly)
with the slow hints of pain.
With Life Savers in our mouths
we still walk the constitutional block;
warm slippers go from here to there, the house
a haven for a slow acrobat;
the *Globe and Mail* as usual
promising all that's necessary
to get by in the world, tips
on civilization, tid-bits on barbarism;
Channel 4, Buffalo, to excite our evenings
with the latest four murders in the city,
and Dan Rather announcing
some sure improvements in the US economy.

It is the slow dying
to your three-year-old son,
hugging you with warm milk
still hot on his breath; to your loving wife
reading to you the relevant ads:
top-soil going at half price and delivered,
Hush Puppies, the star at Eaton's Spring Sale:
to the smell of temperado rice
pappadams,
curried chicken à la Ceylon.

The trouble with growing old
is knowing that dark edge
where we walk with the giggling gait of children,
with the old man certain
of the finality of muscle, the poems
that will never sing or happen again.

LIBRA

The horoscope man
  looks at me floating
under Libra's balancing star
  and says to my mother:

this one
  will surely embrace
the warming word,
  hear the lion roar,
then quickly lie down
  with the lamb.

He'll chase the morning light
  as Apollo Daphne,
refuse
  noon's obtrusive red face
and wait
  for the twilight hours
the raven against a solferino sky,
  to play his moods, his poems
of quiet deliberation.

He'll walk comfortably
  among sinners and saints,
fashion love
  without tragic theatre, touch life
like Beethoven on the keys
  under a haunting moon.

Yes. The poetic juices
  will run, but slowly and sweetly
like the Maple's spring sap,
  and in the end,
he'll go gently into that dark night.

Wrong,
my horoscope man.
  For three score years and five,
there's been no balance for me,

nothing in-between, no fire-side poem
to lullaby the heart, only
hammer and sword,
blood-stained epaulets
on my tunic;
fire in a crystal glass, either
the cobra's sac or a love
that would follow the Christ to Golgotha.

Not for me
morning's blue mist, only
the sun's tight embrace
at high noon; no twilight
when the horizon hemorrhaged
like a wound,
and the bird in flight darkened its wing
too soon, too soon.

I took the dark night,
with only the winking lamps
of the firefly,
the solitude, the poem, the jungle theatre
where the elephant rumbled
at the water hole,
and the staccato squeal of the water hog
was nothing more
than the boisterous order
of life and death.

No. I will not go gently into that dark night.
You'll first hear
the Kandyan drums make fire
under the dancer's anklet bells,
the raven caw the breaking news,
the elephant's last clear trumpet—
and I, wearing the skull cap
of the noonday sun, rosary in hand,
will seek the Kingdom of God,
with the face of a sinner,
and the soul of a faltering saint.

In the Idiom of the Sun

DISTANT RAIN

Your exotic pot
of White Rose hibiscus
has never known the Island sun
or monsoon rain.
So memory for you, my son,
is without green history.

As glass and stone
have framed your dark eyes
and all you know
is that land that falls asleep
in soft white pyjamas
with snowflakes to muffle
its heavy breathing.

I guess you can keep on
asking angrily:
do you have to hang up your story
like a butcher's side of beef?
Why another poem?
Why roll the rock
from mouth of the tomb,
what's there in shadows, dry bones,
memories?

I raise my tired eyes
from the title of a poem
still new, fierce and lamenting:
"The Rain Doesn't Know Me Any More,"
   to remember, to remember
the rain drops
bigger than my childhood eyes,
those blue fists
fast and liquid as a therapist's.

How the good earth churned

its red dust bowl,
burgeoned to a riot of batik,
and the sky caught the colours below
like a memory.

INFANT FOOTFALLS ON RED CEMENT FLOORS

I've left the green land
mother country—
so, what thoughts
will ever silence

the infant footfalls
on red cement floors,
restore the omphalos blood
that sang my green days?

How argue the diaspora?

Would I let nostalgia
flirt with hyperbole?
Is there enough love
to conjure past perfections,
forget, forgive
those strident voices,
the arrhythmia of the wicked heart?

I know. I'll make the coconut tree
straight,
without hint of midnight beetle deep
in the pink fruit's throat.

There's a raging moon,
the fruit bat's nightly orgy is on;
but *cadju-pulang* and mango
will still be whole and sweet
as new-born toddy—
nothing will fester
under this extravagant sun,
the fruit-fly will not feast.

As for the monsoon rain,
there'll only be the beautiful slant

of raindrops,
        cool massage,
me dancing naked
        under God's own shower head;
and the havocking floods,
        mud huts dissolving like chocolate?
bloated bodies
        riding the dark currents to the sea?

I wouldn't know.

From here,
        this imperfect beautiful land,
new entrances seem
        rational, imperative;
old exits survive, ride
        the sweet inventions of memory;
the green land
        forever green,
the lost country
        ever perfect.

BECOMING

When my friend turns his back
   and walks away
and my sad song disappears unsung
   into the thick humid air;

when I watch how the clouds
   quietly shatter my sun's noonday exuberance,
when I hear the cardinal calling, calling, calling
   and no comforting answer rides the twilight air;

when my God finally wakes up
   to my many genuflections, prayers
and turns the lengthening shadows
   to night's sweet closure

to throw its arms
   round my wounded day
and seal the hemophiliac pain
   with its kiss of sleep;

only then
   do I begin to know
how the journey might begin,
how it may end ;

why I must share the bruising plow
   with the tired sun-burnt buffalo,
and let the man becoming

become a man.

CAVEAT

Save me from the silent ones—
those who also claim the untapped wisdom of stones,
whose closed mouths thrive in the open air
as would the blind mole in the bowels of the earth;
how the unsaid word
can kill slowly but surely.
I will not walk in this dark soundless night,
give me a noisy path under a blazing sun,
or twilight sky or even an intransigent moon.

Let not my enemies hold their silences—
for their killing fields
to suggest no strategies, no moments,
but let them rather growl in their rage,
thump their boots,
throw up their clenched fists,
and I'll be ready.

Consider the silence of the cobra in grass,
the thunder of the charging elephant—
how one silently paralyzes its victim
and never waits to hear the last gasp of death
as the other often misses its quarry,
the fleeing limbs, the refuge
in the arms of the closest acacia tree.

I see the insurgent fire
shoot out its vagabond flames,
hear the crackle of roof tops
crumbling to their fiery deaths,
and I discreetly stand back—
but save me
from those unseen embers under ash
quietly awaiting another conflagration,
an appetite   unappeased
for the cruel burn of death.

THE GHOSTS OF KINGS

Does it matter
   if Sheba the lioness at the Dehiwela Zoo
has grown fat with too much sleep
   growls only at dinner time,
lets Juanis, the keeper,
   kiss her occasionally
on her wet nose?

If Gemunu, the Bengal tiger,
   looks harassed and squints,
each eye
   still clotting blood
from a careless hand,
   dreams marrow
from his keeper's thigh bone?

Do you understand
   the ambush at evening, the necessary
sweet menu of death?
   Why diagrams here
are drawn in warm blood and magnificent bone,
   like Sheba's breathless couch,
roped muscles thrown like a lariat,
   the boar's last choking cry,
collapsing thud?

And do you understand
   the sacrament by the waters?
The waterhole's chalice for Gemunu and Sheba
   to sip with the cool arrogance of kings,
where few who dared to drink
   with the anointed, lived,
others, leaking the uncertain nerve,
   provoked new sacrifice,
and the sacrament of life
   was also the fresh smell of death.

Understanding   frees,
  bares the bugger and bitch
in every steel bar
  that fashions the ghosts of kings.

PAST TENSE

This tree   not of the mango
this bird   not of the raven
this river   not the Mahaveli
this moon   not Colombo's halo of blue light
this head of corn   not the sweet rice paddy
this sun   without its embracing arms
this cold   that kills the exotic flesh

exile   you are not
the colour of flesh
that prompts the unkind word,
the prison of accents, basmati rice,
walls that shape
those dark configurations of loneliness

it's the eyes that see
and do not see
the heart that beats
and does not beat

the green land   locked
in the far cold almirahs of memory

"KNOW YOUR OWN BONE"

—Thoreau

Is my heart's passionate dance
  but a moth flirting with the flame?
The long search   sweet discovery,
  you in dream,
the way you walked, walking
  with a temple flower in your hair,
choosing denial, the Belladonna way.

What do I see, or choose to see
  by morning light?
Why does the mind always make choices
  for the eye?
You at the breakfast table,
  dispensing rituals
of Crispix cereal, orange juice, hot milk, and toast;
  I, jousting with clock and laces,
winter boots that seem to shy
  from new journeys into the snow.

Night unravels the knotted muscle,
  makes room for dream, memory
that questions sad exits.
  chases the "whole bloody bird"
and ends up with a feather;
  must I remember the love I couldn't have,
forget the love of those I have?

Why, I ask my bones, is it harder to live
  than to die?
Death in minute doses, small martyrdoms,
  like noon's bland tuna sandwich,
the mailman's choice of junk mail and Christmas bills,
  road salt and arthritis on my snow-shovelling hands,
the body's slow disarmament.

And when I unearth these bones again,
gnaw at them slowly,
my father's riding the mathematical surf
like a beach boy,
as mother nurtures her restless brood of eight
with curried and embracing love,
rattan cane;
I see my wintered children
greening with summer,
my grandson, Jens, throbbing and thriving
in his Viking snows.

Dear Muse,
this bone that lets me suck
the sweet marrow of words,
in mine, stays here, is now—
no damp earth of burial,
no unearthing shovel's bruise;
but why those first gestures
of distrust?
how like a cruel sibling
you once held the candy under my nose,
then snatched it away and laughed.

Now that you've
offered me
the heart of the flute,
be happy for the tapestries of my song,
the raven flies the world;
I hear the immigrant's voice, sweet and clear
as bamboo reed,
the elephant's trumpet
shatter the dark silences
of the snow lands.

MAGPIE

To read
  the palm's dark intersections
  with tea leaves
  or tiny bones that collapse
  in peculiar angles,
  tarot cards,
  the geometry of stars,
  omens of time in one's birth.

No—
  these, they say in the old country,
  are nothing but human fakeries.

Instead
  learn to read
  the magpie's many voices, chattering idiom,
  the harbinger of numbers
  and understand
  the strutting arrogance
  of this black and white prophet.

So if you happen to see a magpie

  alone,
  sorrow's in the air
  if alone, and in the throes
  of a long shrill cry,
  be prepared to bury your dead;
  in twos, it's time for carnival,
  the happy heady rhythms of the *rabana*,
  the smell of temple flowers at the Buddha's feet;

three's for clasping hands,
a wedding feast;
four's a boy! perfect cue
for milk-rice and *katta-sambol*,

the Arrak's coconut fire;
five or more, chattering aimlessly:
life will go
around, riding
the endless carousels.

If life, as they say in the old country,
moves with the karma
of joy and sorrow,
in perfect unison
with the chattering prophecies
of this piebald prophet

why not listen
to the drumbeat of its song,
try to read
its loaded code of numbers?

LOVE POEM FOR ANNE

For you, brown lover,
with buffalo curd and palmyrah honey
still sweet on your lips,
the raven winging in your hair,

I offer the immigrant land
with no contrary season,
only summer
and summer and summer.

No white laming cold before the thaw,
no cutting nodule of spring,
no fallen leaves to confuse your feet,
only the consummate thing,

the full-blown rose, the sun
in batik exuberance.

Now also ask for the sweet warm rain,
the once harvest of fruit:
jambu, mango, and mangosteen;
guava and rambuttan, the tender cadju

wrapped in green leaves, the jiggery bell
of the godambara-rotti man,
and I will tease the Asian condiment
from the summer almirahs of this land.

What you deserve will be
what you always had
in your warm rich blood:

the green land.

THE TWO FACES OF LOVE

If my mother knew
my father knew
that one day
I would trade the land
of eternal summers,

forget the heart of the coconut,
the sea's blue murmurings,
how the elephant loiters
under the wood-apple tree,
lolls in the Heen-Wewa's cool waters

for this winter's numbing furies,
small frame house
with its stuttering faucets,
rusty old furnace,
brown withered roof for hat,

this wind that searches and gnaws
my sun-oiled bones,
this ice-cream snow
that's playground and tombstone,

what would they have said?

Mother: Why, my son, why?
What for, my son, what for?

Father: Go for it, son, go for it!
Even if you must first
fall on your brown face,
endure like cobblestones,
taste your own blood—
frontiers are for crossing!

SIMILES OF DARKNESS

As a black cloud   blindfolds
an August moon

as the muscles of your face tighten
to a shadow with a beating heart

as the spilled ink dooms
the poet's shining new lines

as the cry of the prairie dog
in the sweep of the eagle

as white lightning
ravages the velvet-dark eyes of night

as the blood of the sun
in its twilight journey

as the aphid
in the heart of the rose

as the story in your blue eyes   ends
with the darkness of another man's skin

These Other Configurations

MOVING

When it happens,
and your rooms are finally empty
and bare as bones,
and it's time to step out
from that old ship
of dreams
where you wrote your history
for twenty years and laughed:
  a child sitting on his potty
  pummeling his teddy bear,
  the pappadams hissing and sizzling,
  where buryani and chicken curry
  seduced your Christmas mouths,
  and Santa Claus lumped himself
  on a kitchen chair and went for
  the brandy and eggnog.

What do you say?
What do you keep?

You must know
that the silence of emptiness
is no silence,
it is a wordless thunder,
the hammers of the heart beating
with long-ago laughter,
or stories grave and grieved.

So do not look back
and mourn the moving hour.
What is bare and empty
remains bare and empty
only if the mind lets go
the continuing dream, refuses
memory   history
sitting on the porch at evening
and taking in the evening star.

PASTORAL IN BLUE

Country morning—
pewter clouds
echo of distant thunder
promising nothing
but an unforgiving day;

Mid-afternoon—
no sliver of sun
no joyous sparrow
or robin on grass
only, the seeming lockjaw,
the maple's grim silence;

Evening—
the last raven gone
blood of twilight
nowhere the fireflies
the fruit-bat's
on its way;

Night—
the tree-frog speaks
in woodland patois
as the shadowy pond ripples
to the long legs
of the tadpole;

Then evening's
last soughing of leaves—
a country lullaby
for night's
forgiving sleep.

A TOUCH OF GENETICS

for Michael

Nothing is told
of that which the eyes cannot readily see,
the inexorable genetics of our lives—
my fire now yours, my mind
a hint of precious clone,
how poetry lurks somewhere in your soul
as the Muse keeps whispering about your ears;
where impatience trumps discretion,
a tumbler of water slips
through your careless fingers
and your mother spouts the usual lines:
"Just like your father, clumsy!"
where great love begets great love—
flowers blazing
in the summer sun.

But come those other configurations—
how you trace
your father's face, sun-burnt skin, the name
that makes you heir
to his kingdom of flesh and bone and marrow

and the story is told and told and re-told
how even from behind, my son, they see
your father's slow amble,
the sloping shoulders, brief neck,

and your mother, sweet and joking
at his logic of imperfections,
your father, a fixed star, proud
of this inexhaustible fire, genetics
visualizing nothing
but the traces of his own face, the childish babble
now equal to sheer poetry.

THE PAIN IN THE RICKSHAWMAN'S THIGHS

when it's time for weeping
and we all laugh,

a time for laughing
and we all weep,

a time for living
and we die one by one,

time for the mantra
and our mouths full of ash and stones,

when we choose a breed
of fragmented men,

a world spinning too close to fire,
fashion possibilities

of night suddenly falling
into the morning face of day.

THE PHOTOGRAPH

for Theresa and Phil

of summer's grand effusions,
illusions,
this sheen of coloured plastic
for memory.

This riot of green,
thick grass,
dandelions' dance
to a new summer breeze;

tennis playground
beyond the manicured hedge,
the white winding road   going where ?
to a warm farm house
where love reeks
of pancakes and maple syrup

when a father and son
come walking up the winding road
hand in hand,
their faces now darker
by the summer's dappled shadows;

a tall father,
a son's brief bones,
a father's midnight crown of hair,
a son's blonde coconut head.

  They aren't talking to each other,
  as if talking would crack
  their egg of silence;

but eloquence flows—
those unsaid words,
silent trust,

when hands clasp
and the blood beats
in sweet tandem,

dream that moves,
as they move inch by inch up the road
to a warm cottage porch
where pancakes and maple syrup
await their summer guests.

INHERITANCE

A shaving brush,
its bristles now shrunk and willowed with age;
a tortoise-shell powder box,
some Cuticura talc still stewing in its aroma,
a wasted chamois puff: all these
I asked for and received.

Instruments of my father's morning ablutions,
the body perfect
only when blessed with the scented talc.
The act was defensive, not vain.
He had to take the sweat that swelled
at high noon, lasted
till his teaching was over at four.

Meet the man who was always ready
for life's small disasters.
Once hospitalized
he insisted on packing six candles,
swearing: the damn hospital
will blow a fuse as soon as I arrive.
It did. And there he was
the only heart patient in the golden eye
of candle light.
Telling the story, his round face
would explode with laughter,
his proof of wisdom over folly.
Mother got the house, the few rupees
left in his bank account;
Shakespeare, Milton, the great Romantics,
the mathematical treatises, religious paraphernalia,
Latin and Greek texts,
went to my five brothers and two sisters.

And I?
An old shaving brush,

powder box,
chamois puff.

How well we choose the metaphors of fantastic love,
trinkets that translate the man, his life,
ourselves.
Against the others who took the high road
of his learning, I chose
a rustic byway to his face, his arthritic body.
So what of margins, the synecdoche of flesh?

They frame, throw light
on the center stage, hold
the edges of memory to the sun.
We all have the inherited vein,
the inexorable genetic.
I have more: the old powder box,
one sniff, and he comes alive,
his body perfect, ready
to meet the noonday sun.

IN TRYING TIMES

Only the dream—
no wife, no squawking child,
no dog, no TV chatter,
no thoughts
on my neighbour's Pinnochio nose,
the far ambulance
wailing a near death,
or summer's hot lariat air;

where I am now
on the top of this mountain
where the wind has dropped
and the clouds have given way
to a palavering blue sky
and I see an eagle
riding the rarefied air like an angel
sent from heaven
and the drooping flag of my face, my soul,
now flapping proud
in the sweet breeze
of the cold mountain's breath.

WANTED

Only a love
that will accept
the exotic dream in my head:

hold my darkness
like a magic lantern
against the intruding stars,

see my forehead
as a hurricane lamp refusing
the troubled sea wind;

embrace a love
that's soft as the morning light,
a fire stroked to a slow steady burn;

read time's unfolding answer
not in my aching head,
arthritic hands,

but in the champagne light
dancing
about my fading eyes.

ELEGY FOR AN ORANGE

How your roundness
throbbed to titillate,
your dress of furious saffron
took my eyes;
and your skin,
a snowflake to the touch,
flooded my island of nerves,
collected water in my mouth.

But I could not love you,
I could not seduce you,
I wanted you in totality,
a chemistry of assimilation.
You had to die
tortured for your exotic perfections:
one heave, and I burst you open.
Blood spilled.
I tasted you limb by limb,
wanting you only
in the tongue's orgasm
of your sun-ripe death.

PERSPECTIVES #2

The dead stone
  flung
into the sleeping waters
  throbs and ripples;

the sunflower
  fades and falls
to good earth
  seeding another beginning;

most men
  who falter and fall
ride the crying wound
  to their own resurrection,

and every love
  won and lost
discovers the melody
  of another beautiful song;

every word
  that spills and splatters
in the thatched hut
  sings with a haunting soul;

the cobra
  masks his dance of death
with hisses and slides
  to the snarl of mongoose teeth,

and every laugh
  that cracks the smoking pub
masks an incessant weeping
  in some far other place;

and sometimes the poem
  that's seemingly whole
betrays a virus
  that breaks the poetic code.

SUNLESS SEQUENCES

Today I write of quagmires,
deep fissures, of dreams
that spill blood thick as oil,
Vespers from the mouth of insurgent angels.
You stagger with an exaggerated face,
a knee bone soft as pulp.
What whirls the blood to epilepsy,
so darkens the skyline
as if to frame another crucifixion?

My God, the rose has waited in vain;
the butterfly is changing its ballerina mode
to a clumsy tumble of death.
It is the fourth day
and you hug your doll of flame
like a selfish child
to your ribcage, beyond
our asking eyes, cold skins,
your cumulus curtain drawn tight,
as if for another siesta.

FLIGHT OF THE WHITE BUTTERFLY

O Lord,   why?
why did you let her go
in immaculate wings   alone
into this last day of summer,
this field
that already sniffs
the coming of gusting thieves?

Where only the sun keeps
its red adolescence,
the buttercups sway
thinly pale, the lone pussy-willow
droops with age,
and the fallen apples ferment
through their gnawed skins.

Where the grass
now curls in ruin,
and the distant elms hold on
to their moods,
silent sentinels,
waiting
for the shame of nakedness.

Into this slipping audience,
you send her dancing,
tiny white ballerina
on a cushion of air,
minute bones all summer-oiled
for magnificent performance,
to contradict
these farewell moods, despair.

To boast
of the delicate lace round her body:
milk wings that riot

among the bleeding sumac;
to kiss the dandelions to blush,
doodle on the sky's absolute blue,
for the sun to catch
her white fire like diamonds.

To dance
her last act
to this tambourine of new wind,
to pirouette, cavort, gypsy
through the sunflowers,
arch to the dandelions' wine,
then leap again with the magic
of a prima donna's limbs.

O Lord,   why?
why when the sun
finally closed its red eyes,
did you let her go   alone
into the dark elms for ever?
Did you prime her soft wings
to the catechism of a season,

to dance.
to die,
to end this voluptuous summer?

Acknowledgements

Some of these poems first appeared in the following journals: *The New York Quarterly, The Toronto Review, The Malahat Review, Fiddlehead, Quarry, Globe and Mail, Canadian Literature, Prism International, Ariel, Descant.*

My warm thanks to all those who helped me in this project, especially Bryan Smith, Chelva Kanaganayakam, Tissa Abeysekara, and Andrew Stubbs. As always, my thanks to my son, Michael, for his cover design.